빈집
Empty House

빈집
Empty House

백승연(Baek Seong-yeon) 시집
번역 최재진(Jay Choi), Danielle Scott

신세계문학

시인의 말

지난여름은 길고 뜨거웠다.
먼 나라에서는 전쟁이 끝날 듯
끝나지 않았고 젊은 청춘들은
휩쓸리듯 산화되어 갔다.
덩달아 평화롭게 살던 일반
시민들도 죽어갔다.
어느 드라마의 늙은 주인공이
"내 몸뚱이가 역사랑 게"
하던 문장이 생각난다.
살고 보니 내 몸도
역사의 중요한 순간순간을
살아온 듯하다.

Poet's Words

Last summer was long and hot.
In distant lands, wars seemed to end
yet did not, and young souls
were swept away, consumed like flames.
Even ordinary citizens, living peacefully,
perished alongside them.
I recall a line from an old drama's protagonist:
"My body is tied to history."
Living through it, it feels as though
my own body has walked
through pivotal moments of history.

차례

1부 | 일상의 불씨 · Embers of the Everyday

시인의 말 · 4
Poet's Words · 5

가을날 오후 3시에는 · 12
At Three in the Afternoon on an Autumn Day · 14
겨울 잠행 · 16
Winter Seclusion - Candlelight · 18
동백꽃 · 20
Camellia · 21
목련 · 22
Magnolia · 23
물안개 · 24
Water Mist · 26
별일 없었다 · 28
Nothing Much Happened · 30
빈집 · 32
Empty House · 33
아메리카타운 · 34
America Town · 36
영화동에는 지금 榮華가 없다 · 38
There Is No Glory in Yeonghwa-dong Now · 41
오식도 1 · 45
Osikdo 1 · 47
파꽃만 핀 집 · 49
The House Where Only Green Onions Bloom · 50
풍선을 든 여인 2 · 51
Woman with a Balloon 2 · 53
한 여자 · 55
One Woman · 57

2부 | 마음의 조수(潮水) · Tides of Heart

가뭄 · 60
Drought · 61
강은 저 홀로 · 62
The River · 63
능소화의 일몰 · 54
The Sunset of the Trumpet Vine · 65
돌매 · 67
Stoning · 69
물의 저녁 · 71
The Evening of Water · 72
빗물 · 73
Rainwater · 74
사막을 건너는 법 · 75
How to Cross the Desert · 76
석류를 보며 · 77
While Looking at the Pomegranate · 79
여름 해변 · 81
Summer Beach · 82
오동꽃 필 때 · 83
When the Paulownia Flowers Bloom · 84
장마 · 85
Monsoon · 87
저 석양의 단풍나무 좀 봐 · 89
Look at that maple tree in the sunset · 90
철쭉 빛 저고리 · 91
The Azalea-Colored Jacket · 92
첫눈 · 93
Silver Birds Descend · 94
청(靑) · 95
Blue · 97

3부 | 바람의 속삭임 · Whispers in the Wind

가을 산 · 100
Autumn Mountain · 101
가을 소리 · 102
The Sound of Autumn · 103
갈대 · 104
Galdae · 105
그 섬에는 바람이 · 106
On that island, the wind · 107
눈의 정원 · 108
The Garden of Snow · 110
만추 · 112
Late Autumn · 114
엉겅퀴꽃 · 116
Thistle Flower · 118
여름 바다 · 120
Summer Sea · 121
여름 환(幻) · 122
Summer Illusion · 124
저물녘 산사에서 · 126
At the Mountain Temple in the Twilight · 127
지는 목련꽃 · 128
The Fading Magnolia Blossom · 129
찔레꽃 언덕 · 130
The Briar Rose Hill · 131
칠월 푸른 숲 · 132
Blue Forest of July · 134
파밭길 · 136
Green Onion Field Path · 137
푸름에 대하여 · 138
On Blueness · 139

4부 | 엉켜진 대지 · Woven Earth

가을 연가 · 142
Autumn Love Song · 144
가을 환(幻) · 146
Autumn Illusion · 147
넝쿨 · 148
Vine · 150
덕진 연못에 핀 연꽃 · 152
The Lotus in Deokjin Pond · 154
무꽃 · 156
Radish Flower · 157
밤 부둣가 · 158
Night at the Wharf · 159
변산 바람꽃 · 160
Byeonsan Windflower · 162
실잠자리 · 164
Dragonfly · 165
어은리 염전 · 166
Eoun-ri Salt Field · 167
초봄 · 169
Early spring · 170
폭우 · 171
Torrential Rain · 173
현(絃) · 175
String · 176

발문 · Appreciation
오후 3시의 상상력: 백승연의 시와 실존의 사막 _ 최재진 · 178
The Imagination of Three in the Afternoon:
Baek Seung-yeon's Poetry and the Desert of Existence _ Jay Choi · 185

제1부

일상의 불씨
Embers of the Everyday

가을날 오후 3시에는

가을날 오후 3시에는
나는 사방이 환한 빛의 외줄을 타고 싶네
아무도 말리지 않는 빛의 외줄을 타고 별보다 멀리
떠오르는 그 무엇이 되어
그 무엇이 되지 못한 나의
그 무엇이 되어
가을날 오후 3시에는
낮은 키로 물구나무서서
그 무엇이 되고 싶었는데
그 무엇이 되지 못한
가을날 오후 3시에는
허(虛)와 실(實)의
기막힌 사유(思惟)의 달마처럼
각인된 존재의 의미로 낙하하고 싶었는데
문득 슬프고도 슬퍼라
온갖 존재의 의미는 생(生)의 문장(文章)위에
초췌한 방점(傍點)을 찍고
쫓기는 시계추 소리에
댕댕 희디흰 문을 걸어나와
나는 가출하고 싶다

집전하는 수도사의 옷자락 뒤에
얌전히 서서
나는 금지된 사랑을 말하고 싶다
정적과 정적이 흐르는 단두대에서
모가지 툭 떨어트린
내란음모죄의 사형수를 사랑했노라고
말하고 싶다
가을날 오후 3시에는

At Three in the Afternoon on an Autumn Day

At three in the afternoon on an autumn day,
I want to ride a tightrope of radiant light,
A tightrope of light that no one forbids,
To go beyond the stars,
Becoming something that rises,
Becoming the something I could not become,
The something I yearned to be.
At three in the afternoon on an autumn day,
Standing on my hands in a low stance,
I wanted to become that something,
That something I could not become.
At three in the afternoon on an autumn day,
Like the Dalma of sublime contemplation,
Between the void and the real,
I wanted to fall as the imprinted meaning of existence.
Yet suddenly, I am sad, so sad,
The meaning of all existence
Places a weary comma
Upon the sentence of life,
And to the sound of a chased clock's pendulum,

Through a stark white door,
I want to run away.
Standing quietly behind the hem
Of a praying monk's robe,
I want to speak of forbidden love.
At the guillotine where silence flows,
I want to declare my love
For the condemned traitor whose head was severed.
At three in the afternoon on an autumn day

겨울 잠행
— 촛불

무릎을 꿇어요
팔짱을 껴봐요
가슴을 오므려요
고개를 숙여요
조그맣게 조그맣게
작아져 봐요

침잠하는 어둠 속에
떨며 숨죽이며
꿈의 온몸을 만져요

마음에서 가슴에서
안에서 밖에서
우우 쓰러지는 평화

하나의 조용함이
가득 차올라
당신 속에 내가 있어요

꽝꽝 얼어붙는

겨울밤
스스로 목숨 태워
당신 곁에 내가 빛나요

무엇엔가 홀려 있는 것 같아요
떨쳐낼 수 없는 것 같아요

Winter Seclusion
— Candlelight

I kneel down,
cross my arms,
draw my chest inward,
lower my head,
quietly, so quietly,
I make myself small.

In the submerging darkness,
trembling, holding my breath,
I touch the entirety of a dream.

From the heart, from the chest,
from within, from without,
a peace that collapses with a sigh.

A single stillness
rises to fill the space,
and I am within you.

On a frozen winter night,

burning my own life,
I shine beside you.

It feels like I'm enchanted by something,
something I cannot shake off.

동백꽃

해거름 녘엔
떨고 있다

대웅전 한켠에
쪼그리고 앉아
한차례 밭은 기침하며
기울어진 달

단애(斷崖) 위를 걸어가듯
가슴에 접어둔 사랑아

지난밤부터
차마 전하지 못한 소식
해풍에 뒤챈다

Camellia

At twilight,
it trembles.

Crouched in a corner
of the great hall,
coughing once,
beneath a tilting moon.

Like walking along a cliff's edge,
oh, the love folded in my heart.

Since last night,
news I couldn't bear to share
is tossed by the sea breeze.

목련

꽃이여
숨은 날개 폈구나
몇몇 외로운 날의
낯빛 감추고
막막히 서 있던 나무여
눈바람 뒤집어쓴 채
쓰린 결별을 목놓아 울던 바람이여
겨울 문 곁에서 죽음 보낸
오들오들 떨던 시간의 틈으로
꽃 시간은 오고 있느냐
가끔씩 생각이 그리운 날에는
분홍빛 이름 부르다가 겨울은 갔다
한 장 한 장 손수건 접어
새벽 창가에 놓아두면
첫 기차
떠나기 전
봄의 정령들은 손수건을 물고
꽃소식 퍼뜨리는구나

Magnolia

Oh flower,
you've unfurled your hidden wings.
The tree that stood desolate,
hiding the pallor of lonely days,
and the wind, keening through bitter farewells,
cloaked in stinging snowstorms.
From the crevice of trembling time,
having sent death away at winter's gate,
is the hour of flowers approaching?
On days when thoughts turn to longing,
calling out your pink-hued name,
winter has departed.
Folding handkerchiefs one by one,
placing them by the dawn's window,
before the first train leaves,
the spirits of spring clutch those handkerchiefs
and spread the tidings of flower.

물안개

들어보세요
날마다 날마다
내 발목으로 차오르는 물소리를
들어보세요

지난밤 험한 산줄기 타고 내려온
찬 이슬이
내 뜨거운 이마에
푸른 우수의 알갱이로 떠돌 때
나는 그대 곁을 서성이며
가만가만 발돋음하였어요

한없이 풀어놓은
푸른 우수의 그림자들은
팔락팔락 나부끼며
그대 꿈의 갈피에 스며들고 싶었나 봐요

도시의 옥상에, 도시의 골목에,
도시의 네온사인에, 도시의 가로등에
깊이 잠든 시민들의 잠 속에 살풋 맴돌다

최종적으로 머물고 싶은 곳은 어디일까요

목줄기를 훑고 지나가는
가벼운 바람의 느낌이
대기의 체온이
하늘에 걸린 흰 띠의 입자로 다가와
그대의 머리에 그대의 이마에 그대의
눈에 그대의 가슴에

내가 차마 전할 수 없는 밀어를
구슬로 꿰어 전하고 싶었나 봐요

Water Mist

Listen,
Day after day,
The sound of water rising to my ankles—
Listen.

The cold dew that descended last night
Along the rugged mountain ridges
Hovers as beads of blue melancholy
On my fevered forehead.
I lingered by your side,
Quietly standing on tiptoe.

The shadows of blue melancholy,
Endlessly unfurled,
Flutter and sway,
Longing to seep into the folds of your dreams.

On the city's rooftops, in its alleys,
On its neon signs, its streetlights,
Softly circling through the dreams of sleeping citizens,

Where is it that they finally wish to rest?
The feeling of a gentle breeze

Brushing past your throat,
The warmth of the air,
Approaching as particles of a white ribbon hung in the sky,
To your head, your forehead,

Your eyes, your heart—
The secret words I could not dare to speak,
I must have wanted to string them like beads
And offer them to you.

별일 없었다

발끝에 슴슴한 기운이 스멀거렸다

마을 입구에 들어서면
버들잎 휘늘어진 봄의 입술이 빵긋거리고
집집마다 닫혔던 창문을 열고, 탈탈
묵은 먼지 터는 소리 소란했다

어디선가 백목련 향 내음 스밀 때
산 마을을 내려다보면
겨울은 꽁꽁 얼어붙은 내장을 꺼내놓아
젖은 몸을 말렸다

솜털 보송한 쑥잎 돋아나는 텃밭으로
텃새들 포로롱 날아간 발끝에 아지랑이 남실남실
내리비치는 햇살 따라 우리들은 두터운 외투를 벗었다

가볍고 부드러운 옷으로 갈아입을 즈음
우리들 고관절 통증도 풀리고
몸은 날아갈 듯 가벼웠다
그리고 봄이었다

겨울과 봄의 경계에서 우리들은 별일 없었다

Nothing Much Happened

A faint chill lingered at my toes.

At the village entrance,
The lips of spring, willow leaves drooping, smiled softly.
From every house, windows long shut were flung open,
The clamor of shaking out old dust filled the air.

When the scent of magnolia wafted from somewhere,
Looking down on the mountain village,
Winter laid bare its frozen innards,

Drying its damp body.
In the garden where soft, fuzzy mugwort leaves sprouted,
Birds flitted away, leaving shimmers of heat haze at their toes.
Following the slanting sunlight, we shed our heavy coats.

As we changed into light, soft clothes,
The ache in our joints eased,
Our bodies felt light enough to fly.
And it was spring.

At the boundary of winter and spring,
Nothing much happened to us.

빈집

바람이 시도 때도 없이 훑고 지나갔겠지

창문이 열리고 방문이 열리고
대문이 열리고
마침내 바람에 몽땅 털린 세간살이

사람의 온기까지
트럭 채 싣고 떠나버린
바람 숭숭한 집

다시 창문이 닫히고 방문이 닫히고
대문이 닫히고 대문 밖 자물쇠로 마무리된
울 밖으로 나팔꽃이 꿈처럼 피어있다

바람 따라 날아온 나팔 꽃씨 하나

베란다 난간에
간신히 터 잡고 싹을 틔워
나팔나팔 햇살 따라
고개 돌리며 주인 행세를 한다

Empty House

The wind must have swept through at all hours,

rattling the windows open, the doors ajar,
the front gate unlatched,
until every household item was stripped bare by the gusts.

Even the warmth of human presence
was loaded onto a truck and carried away,
leaving a house hollow with wind.

The windows close again, the doors shut tight,
the front gate locked outside,
and beyond the fence, morning glories bloom like a dream.

A single morning glory seed,
carried by the wind,

barely takes root on the balcony railing,
sprouting and swaying,
turning its head to follow the sunlight,
acting as if it owns the place.

아메리카타운

원래는 여기를 떠나려고 했어요
밤마다 멀리 바닷가에선 파도가 일렁이고
가끔 비행장에서 굉음을 던지며
아메리카 비행기가 떴어요
우리는 이 고장에서
바람을 못 이겨 움막을 쳤더랬어요
피난 오느라 열흘쯤 굶었더랬어요
우리는 참을 수 없는 배고픔을 참으면서
서로 움푹 들어간 눈망울을
그냥 바라볼 수밖에 없었어요
주인집 처마 밑에 웅크리고 앉아
하늘 높이 떠가는 비행기에
주먹질이나 하는 나날이었어요
가끔 지나가는 양키가 던져준 비스켓이나
초코렛을 먹다 보면 구역질 하느라
더 허천났지요
판자벽 틈으로 알알이 굴러다니는
감자를 훔쳐서 생으로 먹기도 했어요
이 주인집엔 왠 양키들이 밤마다 들락거릴까
우리처럼 많은 피난민들이 곳곳에 움막을 치고

허천난 눈동자를 굴리고 있었어요
마침내 제일 예쁜 우리 큰 언니에게
주인집 여자가 뭐라고 귀속말을 하자
우리 언니는
침대만 커다랗게 차지한 방으로 들어갔어요

America Town*

We had planned to leave this place.
At night, waves rippled far off by the seaside,
and sometimes, from the airfield,
American planes roared into the sky.
In this town,
we built shacks, unable to withstand the wind.
Fleeing here, we starved for about ten days.
Enduring unbearable hunger,
we could only stare into each other's sunken eyes.
Crouching under the eaves of the landlord's house,
we shook our fists at the planes soaring high above.
Sometimes, eating biscuits or chocolate
tossed by passing Yankees,
we retched, feeling even hungrier.
Through cracks in the wooden walls,
we stole potatoes, eating them raw.
Why did so many Yankees come and go
at the landlord's house every night?
Like us, many refugees built shacks here and there,
their famished eyes darting around.

Finally, when the landlord's wife whispered something
to our prettiest older sister,
she entered a room
where a huge bed took up all the space.

*America Town refers to the entertainment district for U.S. military personnel stationed in the Gunsan area where the poet resides.

영화동에는 지금 榮華가 없다

길을 걸어가다 보면 그냥 막막한 숨이나 한번 쉬어 볼 일이다

흐릿한 기억의 저편
바다에선 세찬 바람이 불고 부두의 끝에는 군대 막사 같은
네모진 창고들이 주욱 늘어서 있었다
그 무렵 창고 앞 쌀벌레들은 식민의 아들딸들보다 더 쉽게
쌀 창고 문지방을 넘나들어 차라리 쌀벌레가 부러웠었다

저벅거리던 군화발과 함께 게다짝 소리 딸깍대며 걸어가던
기모노 여인의 아그작거림이 잊혀지기도 전
우리 언니는 양공주가 되고
우리를 지켜주어야 할 국부는 안심하고 기다리라며
도망가 버린 후 안심하고 기다릴 수 없어
총을 든 우리 아빠는 인민군에게 사로잡혀 총살당했다

엄마와 큰 언니, 작은 언니, 나
아빠를 잃은 서울이 무서워 군산으로 피난 내려와
피난살이에 서럽고 밥이 없어 서럽던 그 때
굶다가 굶다가 영 배가 고프면 냉수를 한사발씩 마시다가
피난민 임시 막사 밖으로 나와 엉덩이를 까고 오줌을 누었다

밥도 안 준다며 엄마만 철없이 달달 볶던 날
열아홉 살 우리 큰언니는 입술을 빨갛게 칠하고 카바레에 나갔다
그 후 땡까땡까 땐스홀과 미스터 로버트와 쪼코렛과 토스트와
추잉껌과 함께 먹을 것이 넘쳐났다

여기저기 작은 문을 밀치고 큰 키의 양키들이
레이션박스를 들고 들락거릴 때
땅콩만한 여자들이 살고 있는 방을
기웃 들여다볼라치면 커다란 침대만
한가득 방을 차지하고 있었다

큰언니가 로버트를 닮은 파란 눈의 여자아이를 낳던 날
"엄마! 저앤 예수님을 닮은 것 같아,
언니는 예수의 딸을 낳았나 봐."
하도 엄청나서 쫑알대니까 엄마는 나를 확 밀쳐버렸다

큰언니는 로버트와 함께 우리의 선망의 땅 아메리카로 떠나고
둘째 언니도 덩달아 국제선 타고 떠난 후 구순을 넘긴
엄마와 나는 수입품 가게를 운영하며 영화동에 살고 있다

영화동은 지금 일본인 거리도 미국인 거리도 아닌
일본인 미국인들뿐만 아니라 중국인들까지
북적거리다 떠난 패전국처럼 고요하고 고요할 뿐이다

There Is No Glory in Yeonghwa-dong* Now

Walking down the road,
all you can do is let out a heavy, aimless sigh.

On the far side of hazy memories,
a fierce wind blew from the sea,
and at the end of the pier,
square warehouses stood in a row like army barracks.
Back then, rice weevils crossed the thresholds of rice storehouses
more easily than the sons and daughters of the colony,
and I envied those weevils.

Before I could forget the clacking of wooden clogs
and the rustling of a kimono-clad woman walking alongside
the trudging sound of military boots,
my older sister became a yanggongju,
and the national father, who was supposed to protect us,
told us to wait in peace, then fled.

Unable to wait in peace,
my father, bearing a gun, was captured by the People's Army and shot.

Mother, big sister, little sister, and I—
afraid of Seoul, where we lost Father,
we fled to Gunsan as refugees.
In those days, heartbroken by displacement and hungry for rice,
when starvation gnawed, we gulped down bowls of cold water.
Outside the temporary refugee shelters,
we squatted, bared our hips, and relieved ourselves.

On days when I childishly pestered Mother,
complaining she didn't even give us rice,
my nineteen-year-old big sister painted her lips red
and went to the cabaret.
After that, with the ding-a-ling of the dance hall,
Mr. Robert, chocolate, toast,

and chewing gum, food overflowed.

When tall Yankees pushed through small doors,
carrying ration boxes, coming and going,
I peeked into rooms where women small as peanuts lived,
and saw only enormous beds
filling the entire space.

The day my big sister gave birth to a blue-eyed girl who looked like Robert,
"Mom! She looks like Jesus,
like big sister gave birth to Jesus's daughter."
I chattered in awe, and Mom pushed me away.
Big sister left for America, the land of our dreams, with Robert,
and second sister, caught up in the tide, boarded an international flight too.
Now, past ninety, Mom and I run an import shop,
living in Yeonghwa-dong.

Yeonghwa-dong is no longer a Japanese street nor an American street,
but a place where Japanese, Americans, and even Chinese
once bustled and then left,
now quiet, only quiet, like a defeated nation.

＊Yeonghwa-dong refers to a district in Gunsan. It has the same pronunciation as a Korean word meaning prosperity.

오식도 1

모든 건 흰 배경이다
배경의 배면에 갈매기들 날아오르고
미래는 꿈이겠지

한때 오래오래 산 흔적
가늠할 수 없는 부끄러움으로
갈대들 소리내어 울면

드디어 바람의 몸이 되어
우뚝 선 그대

나는 바람의 손을 잡고
몇 해 째
잔솔가지 많은 언덕을 헤매었다

푸른 귀를 세워
아련히 연안에 닿았다

아침저녁
방파제 둑길로

안개 내린 날

한길로 걸어가서
흙바람에 거칠어진
섬의 피부를 쓸어내려야겠다

Osikdo* 1

Everything is a white background.
On the back of the backdrop, seagulls soar,
and the future must be a dream.

Traces of a life long lived,
with immeasurable shame,
the reeds cry out in sound.

Finally, becoming the body of the wind,
you stand tall.

Holding the hand of the wind,
for years,
I wandered the hills thick with pine branches.

Raising blue ears,
I faintly reached the shore.

Morning and evening,
on foggy days

along the breakwater path,

I must walk the single road
and brush the roughened skin of the island,
worn by the dusty wind.

 *Osikdo is a district in Gunsan where the poet resides; it was once an island but has now been reclaim

파꽃만 핀 집

집마다 장미 넝쿨 호사한 동네 어귀에
파꽃만 핀 집이 있어요
눈치 보며 들어선 마당에
파꽃 냄새 가득

소망처럼 별을 이고 서서
톡톡 영글고 있어요

어디선가 개 한 마리
컹컹 짖고
깨끗이 빨아 널은 옥양목 호청에서
눈부신 유년이 파닥파닥
날개를 치다가

내 소꿉친구의
민둥머리 기계충 같은
단순한 슬픔을 불러와 낙인을 찍어요

The House Where Only Green Onions Bloom

In a neighborhood adorned with rose vines at every house,
There's a house where only green onions bloom.
Stepping cautiously into its yard,
The scent of green onions fills the air.

Standing beneath the stars, like a wish,
They ripen, bursting softly.

Somewhere, a dog barks,
Woof, woof,
And from the cleanly washed, hung cotton cloth,
A dazzling childhood flutters,
Beating its wings.

It calls forth the simple sorrow
Of my childhood friend's
Bald, mechanical heart,
And brands it with a mark.

풍선을 든 여인 2

여인은 불쑤세미 같은 머리를 쳐들고
풍선을 분다

부풀린 풍선 속에 보이는
하늘, 구름, 바람, 비

툴툴거리며 뽀얀 먼지를 한 줌 쏟아놓고 가버린
버스 뒤꽁무니에 아이들은 알밤을 먹으며
재잘재잘 그 뒤를 쫓아간다
한차례 빗줄기가 지나가고, 다시
아무 일도 없었던 것처럼 쏟아지는 눈부신 햇살 아래
풋콩은 익고 풋콩 줄기에서 피고 있는 풋콩 꽃

토끼풀
넝쿨 뻗으며 네 잎 행운을 어디에 꼭꼭 숨겨놓았을까

행운의 먼발치에서 유리구두에 발을 넣으면
하늘 속 마알간 옛날
무좀으로 뒤틀린 발가락이 꼼지락대며
세상의 풍선을 툭 터트린다

펑펑 터지는 이완의 세계에서
슬픔의 액즙을 들이킬까

딸꾹딸꾹

오래도록 딸꾹질에 시달린 삶의 필름이 끊길 때쯤
칠색 무지개의 텅 빈 동공 속에
둥둥 떠도는 하늘, 구름, 바람, 비

Woman with a Balloon 2

The woman lifts her scrub-brush hair
And blows into a balloon.

Visible within the inflated balloon:
Sky, clouds, wind, rain.

Grumbling, the bus scatters a handful of white dust
And departs. Children, feeding it chestnuts,
Chatter and chase after its tail.
After a burst of rain passes,
As if nothing happened, under the dazzling sunlight,
Green beans ripen, green bean flowers bloom on their vines.

Clover,
Stretching its tendrils, where has it hidden its four-leaf luck?

At the far edge of fortune, slipping a foot into a glass slipper,
In the clear, ancient sky,
Toes twisted with athlete's foot wriggle,
Popping the world's balloon.

In the bursting, explosive world of release,
Shall we drink the sap of sorrow?

Hiccup, hiccup.

When the film of a life tormented by endless hiccups finally breaks,
In the empty pupils of a seven-colored rainbow,
Sky, clouds, wind, and rain drift aimlessly.

한 여자

한 여자가 보도블럭에 앉아 있다
자기 안방인양 안심하고 무릎도
얌전히 앉아 있다
그늘 얼추 내려 비치는 행길가에
뒤축이 닳아빠진 구두 두 짝을
여자가 앉은 그늘 속에 가지런히 놓아두고
뜻도 없이 가끔 웃고 있다

때때로 사람들은 그 여자의
시선 속으로 스쳐 지나가고
도시의 복판으로 차량들은 질주한다
철사처럼 뻣뻣한 여자의 머리칼을 흔들면
엉겨 붙었던 파리 떼 윙 날아오르고
여자의 시선 속에 확대된 사람들은
타인이다

시간이 태엽을 풀고 도르르 말려 올라간다
혼을 놓아버린 여자는 연신 방실거리고
여자는 다시 생긋 웃는다
한 남자가 그의 애인에게 주려던

프리지아 꽃다발 속에서 꽃을 꺾어
그 여자의 머리에
장난처럼 꽂고 지나간다

One Woman

A woman sits on a sidewalk block,
As if in her own living room, at ease,
Knees neatly tucked.
In the shade roughly cast along the path,
Two worn-out shoes, heels ground down,
Are neatly placed beside her in the shadow,
And she smiles now and then, without reason.

At times, people pass through
The frame of her gaze,
While cars race through the heart of the city.
When the breeze stirs her stiff, wire-like hair,
A swarm of clinging flies buzzes up,
And the people magnified in her eyes
Are strangers.

Time unwinds its spring and rolls back up.
The woman, lost in her thoughts, keeps giggling,
And smiles softly again.
A man, plucking a flower from a freesia bouquet

Meant for his lover,
Playfully tucks it into her hair
And passes by.

제2부

마음의 조수(潮水)
Tides of Heart

가뭄

 한 점 가려줄 수 있는 그늘 아쉬워 날름 언덕바지로 뛰어 내렸어요
 논두렁에 매달린 날콩들이 쪼르르 굴러떨어지며 단단한 입술을 깨물고, 혓바닥에 고인 마지막 침샘 속의 침을 아껴보지만 갈라진 혓바닥은 어쩔 수가 없어요. 물기라곤 전혀 없는 혀의 굴헝으로 천애의 고독한 말씀들이 쏟아져도, 말씀들은 다만 허공중의 메아리일 뿐이어요. 사방에 먼지만 풀풀 날려요 혀를 길게 빼내 물고 천리 밖 가장 낮은 바다에 촉수를 꽂고 귀를 기울여 보고, 흐르는 물, 물의 숨소리를 듣고 싶어요 어쩔까요. 쟁쟁한 햇살, 유리로 그은 듯한 빛, 초록인 숲을 갈색 숲으로 탈바꿈 시킬듯한 무더위, 그 끝에서 바람은 불까요? 불겠죠. 그 끝으로 빗방울이 후두둑후두둑 떨어질까요?

Drought

Longing for a patch of shade to shield a single moment,
I race down to the hillside's edge.
Field beans, clinging to the ridge, spill in a cascade,
their tight lips bitten,
hoarding the last drops of saliva in parched glands.
Yet my cracked tongue falters, helpless.
Through the dry furrows of its barren folds,
words of desolate solitude pour forth,
only to echo hollowly in the void.
Dust swirls, clouding the air around me.
I extend my tongue, gripping it tightly,
reaching tendrils into the lowest earth, a thousand miles away,
straining to hear—
yearning for the murmur of flowing water, its living breath.
What can I do?
The sun's relentless glare, light etched like glass,
and a heat that could transmute green woods to amber—
will a breeze stir at its end?
It must.
Will raindrops, at last, come pattering down?

강은 저 홀로

강은
저 홀로
깊어지는 이유를 알아요

발끝부터 머리끝까지
눈부신 빛과 소리의
화음으로 흘러요

긴 겨울
은둔의 잠 깨우고
흔들어 일으킨
하늘의 열림이어요

우리 힘껏
껴안긴
온몸의 울림이어요

The River

The river
knows why
it deepens alone.

From the tips of my toes
to the crown of my head,
it flows with the harmony
of dazzling light and sound.

Awakening
from the long winter's
secluded slumber,
it is the opening of the heavens,
stirring and rising.

It is the resonance
of our wholehearted embrace,
the trembling of our entire being.

능소화의 일몰

　난간을 타고 내려오는 길에 그대를 만났습니다
　황혼을 등지고 등피를 닦는 고독한 파수꾼처럼 그대는 등 구부정히 노을을 바라보고 있었습니다
　어떤 고요의 멈춤 속에 낯선 사물이 먹물에 잠긴 듯 그렇게 서 있었습니다
　그때 나는 서산으로 넘어가는 빛의 잔영에 그림자를 길게 늘어뜨리고 거기에 몸을 의탁한 채 바람에 흔들렸습니다. 고단한 생의 옹이로 매듭진 그대의 닳고 닳은 손바닥에 투두둑 떨어진 물의 숨소리가 그대에게 다가갑니다
　연장통을 들고 하루의 일과를 끝마친 그대의 등은 더욱 휘어지고 바람은 완강하게 버틴 그대의 온몸을 휘익 밀치고 달아납니다
　무엇이 그대를 완강하게 버틸 수 있는 침묵의 둘레로 칭칭 감아놓았을까요,
　그립다 못해 애절한 꽃등을 바알갛게 밝히는 나의 순정은 마지막 꺼져가는
　애증의 나팔수가 되려는 준비를 합니다

The Sunset of the Trumpet Vine

On the path descending along the railing, I met you.
Like a solitary sentinel polishing a lantern against the twilight,
you stood, back hunched, gazing at the sunset.
In some stillness of pause, you stood as if a strange object submerged in ink.
At that moment, I let my shadow stretch long in the afterglow of light sinking behind the western hills,
swaying in the wind, entrusting my body to it.
The sound of water's breath, dripping onto your worn, calloused palms,
knotted with the hardships of life, approaches you.
Carrying a toolbox, your back bends further after the day's labor,
and the wind, unyielding, pushes past your steadfast body and flees.
What is it that wraps you tightly in the silent circle of endurance?
My pure longing, burning red with the fervor of a flower lantern,

too yearning to be mere affection,
prepares to become the final trumpeter
of love and hate, fading into the last embers.

몰매

앞 강물 버드나무 가지에
햇살이 부서지고 있었다

나보다 일찍 일어난 아이들은
재잘재잘 들떠서 떠들었다

늦잠에서 깨어나 눈 비비고
하품을 늘어지게 하다가 본
강물은 온몸을 뒤틀었다

들뜬 아이들 손가락 틈 사이로
아이 팔뚝만한 구렁이가 버드나무 가지를
칭칭 휘어감고 있었다

전날 밤 폭풍이 지나간 아침은 눈부셨다
눈부신 햇살 아래 은비늘이 몸을 풀었다

아아! 아이들은 탄성을 지르고
버드나무 가지가 휘청 흔들렸다

한 아이가 돌멩이를 쥐었다
그가 던진 돌멩이가 공중을 날아
버드나무 가지 사이로 비상하는 동안
작은 고요가 햇빛을 찰랑 흔들었다

구렁이는 조금도 서둘지 않고
잎이 무성한 버드나무 몸통으로
슬슬 숨어 올라가고 있었다

아이들은 나도나도 하는 듯 돌팔매질을 했다
흙탕물로 뒤엉킨 강물은
온몸을 뒤틀면서 제 몸을 던져 흘렀다

폐병쟁이 깡마른 자기 남자를 제쳐두고
열 살이나 어린 남자를 꼬드긴 한 여자가
팔매질을 당하고 있었다

Stoning

By the river's willows,
sunlight shattered on the branches.
Children, awake before me,
chattered with giddy excitement.
Waking from a late slumber, rubbing my eyes,
yawning lazily, I saw
the river twisting its entire body.
Between the gaps of the children's fingers,
a snake, thick as a child's arm,
coiled tightly around the willow branches.
The morning after the storm's passing was dazzling.
Beneath the blinding sunlight, silver scales unwound.
Oh! The children gasped in awe,
and the willow branches swayed heavily.
One child gripped a stone.
As the thrown stone soared through the air,
flying between the willow branches,
a small silence rippled the sunlight.
The snake, unhurried,
slipped slowly into the leafy willow trunk,

climbing upward.
The children, one after another, hurled stones.
The river, tangled in muddy waters,
writhed and flung itself forward.
A consumptive, gaunt man cast aside,
a woman who seduced a boy ten years younger
was being pelted with stones.

물의 저녁

물의 그늘이 점점 어둠에 잠겨
물밑으로 스며들 듯 갯바람 불어온다
오래 머물렀을 폐선(廢船)의 유리 밖은
갈매기 날아간 얼룩이 썰물처럼 번져가고
어둠의 바닷길에 부대낀 검푸른 흔적들
물속으로 가라앉는 저녁

죽은자의 언어로 파도가 밀려오면
생전에 다쳤던 슬픔이 되살아나 하얗게 포말(泡沫) 할 때
훌쩍이는 생명의 희디흰 물소리
낮 동안 물 밖의 태양을 온몸으로 받아들이느라
증발한 짜디짠 갯벌의 소금 사리만 남아
황혼의 치맛자락 질질 끌고 간다

The Evening of Water

The shadow of the water, gradually submerged in darkness,
Seeps beneath as the tidal breeze blows in.
Outside the glass of the long-anchored ship,
The stains of gulls' flight spread like the ebbing tide,
And the deep blue traces, battered along the dark sea path,
Sink into the water's evening.

When waves roll in with the language of the dead,
The sorrows wounded in life revive, frothing white.
The sobbing sound of life's pale, white water,
Having absorbed the sun outside the water all day long,
Leaves only the evaporated salt of the briny tidal flats,
Dragging the hem of twilight's skirt as it goes.

빗물

참고 참아왔다
매정하게
날 버리고 떠난 님
억겁의 슬픔이 가슴에 맺혀
한(恨) 덩어리 사무쳤다

앉아 있어도
서 있어도
잠 좀 자보려고 누워 있어도
생각은 깊어지고

돌덩이 하나 가슴에 얹어 놓은 듯
아무리 눌러도 꿈틀 폭발할 것 같은
앙금이 남는다

이윽고
참을 대로 참은 눈물
찔끔찔끔 얼굴을 적시고
옷을 적시며 양철 지붕을
맘껏 두드려 패면서
철철 흘러넘치고 있다

Rainwater

I held it in, held it all back—
the one who cruelly abandoned me,
leaving an eternity of sorrow
to clot into a lump of resentment in my heart.

Sitting,
standing,
lying down to try and sleep,
my thoughts only deepen.

As if a stone were pressed upon my chest,
no matter how I try to suppress it,
a restless, explosive grudge remains.

At last,
the tears I've endured to the breaking point
trickle down, dampening my face,
soaking my clothes,
pounding the tin roof with abandon,
overflowing in torrents.

사막을 건너는 법

뼈와 뼈 사이 열 강열하다
타다닥 뼛속 뜨거움 제풀에 열 받는다
사시사철 소금으로 말라붙은 틈
무거운 멍에 지고 푹푹 빠지는 희디흰 길 뻗친다
살면서 버팅겨준 하늘의 밧줄 칭칭 몸에 휘어 감고
살짝 지나가는 바람에도 흔들려 볼 일이다
풀어내고 풀어내어도 풀리지 않는 인연의 핏줄 끈질긴데
끈질긴 핏줄 산화시킬 사막의 바람 눈물 흘린다
흘린 눈물 빗방울 되어 간식처럼 깔깔하다
걸어도 걸어도 푹푹 빠져드는 모랫더미
굽어진 등 구부리고 허연 머리칼 산발한 여인 엎어진다

How to Cross the Desert

Between bone and bone, the heat blazes fiercely.
The scorching fire within the bones flares up on its own.
A crack, parched and sealed with salt through all seasons,
A blindingly white path stretches, sinking heavily under the weight of a yoke.
Bound tightly by the rope of the sky, endured through a lifetime,
It sways even at the slightest passing breeze.
Though you unravel and unravel, the stubborn thread of fate remains unyielding.
The desert wind, oxidizing that tenacious thread of life, sheds tears.
The tears shed become raindrops, laughing like a snack.
No matter how much you walk, the sand dunes keep swallowing you.
A woman with a bent back, her white hair disheveled, collapses.

석류를 보며

누가 나만큼 그대를
기다린 적 있나
살펴보셨나요

휘휘 휘둘러봐도
무심한 그대에게

꽃 초롱불 밝혀
오시는 길
환히 내어주고 싶었지요

안 오시는 그대

몇 날 며칠 그대 곁을
서성이다가
지쳐 떨어져 내린
꽃등을 아시나요

해가 떠오르면
햇살 한 웅큼

심장에 꾹꾹 눌러
활시위를 당겼습니다

먼발치에서
시간은 흐르고
찬바람 무서리친 가을날
안 오시는 그대

내 생애 가장 아름다운 등을 밝혀
보란 듯이 벙글겠습니다

While Looking at the Pomegranate

Has anyone ever
waited for you as I have?
Have you ever looked?

Even when I whirl and turn,
you remain indifferent.

I wanted to light a flower lantern,
to brightly illuminate
the path for your arrival.

Yet you do not come.

Do you know the flower lamp
that, after lingering by your side
for days and nights,
fell, exhausted?

When the sun rises,
I take a handful of sunlight,

press it firmly into my heart,
and pull the bowstring taut.

From a distance,
time flows on,
and on this autumn day,
frostbitten by the cold wind,
you still do not come.

With the most beautiful lantern of my life ablaze,
I will bloom boldly, as if to show you.

여름 해변

잊은 건 아니어요
청무우 빛 하늘을 이고 오시는 이

푸른 몸피로 서서
혼자만
가만가만 미소 짓지 말아요

지금은 뜨거운 격정을 인내한 채
가장 완전한 기도가 되살아나는 시간

온몸으로 부딪고 스러져
금빛 사건을 긋는
한 마리 새를 기억하셔요

Summer Beach

I haven't forgotten.
You, coming beneath the radish-blue sky.

Standing with a blue body,
don't smile softly
all alone.

Now, enduring fervent passion,
is the time when the most perfect prayer is revived.

Remember the single bird
that crashes with its whole body, falls,
and draws a golden event.

오동꽃 필 때

지금 남아있는 엽신(葉信)가운데
온갖 부드러운 몸짓이
달콤한 훈향을 배풀었을 때
기쁨은 발돋음하고 종을 울렸지

하루씩 창창한 빛 쌓이고
길섶에서 불어오는 바람
가득히 환호하는 눈매로
하늘 열리네

겹겹이 흔들리는 가지에서
밀려오는 꽃 초롱
불 밝히며
그대의 담 모퉁이
창문에 기대어
예감의 시간을 따스히 꿈꾸리

When the Paulownia Flowers Bloom

Among the surviving leaves,
when every tender gesture
spread a sweet fragrance,
joy stood on tiptoe and rang the bell.

Day by day, radiant light piled high,
and the breeze blowing from the roadside,
with eyes full of cheering,
opened the sky.

From the trembling branches, layer upon layer,
flower lanterns surged forth,
lighting up the night.
Leaning against your garden wall's corner,
by the window,
I warmly dream of the time of premonition.

장마

앞산 중턱에
떼 지어 서 있던 물푸레나무
사나흘 건듯건듯 바람 불어오더니
아침부터 흐리고 비가 왔다
종일 비가 왔다

맨방바닥에 맨발바닥을 짚을 때마다
끈적끈적 달라붙는 습기에 온몸이 젖는다

햇빛 맑은 날
그대에게 보송보송 다가갈
화려한 비상을 궁리 중이었더니
오늘 비가 온다

진분홍 백일홍 꽃잎도 젖어서 고개를 숙였다
고개 숙인 것들 어디 백일홍 꽃잎들뿐이랴
결별을 준비한 망설임이 빗물로 흘러간다

망설이지 마라
내가 그토록 그리워한 것들 다 내려놓고

나도 함께 흘러가리라

발끝부터 머리끝까지 젖어서 흘러가리라
그 깊은 물 속
나를 반길 그대에게 온몸 젖어서 흘러가리라

Monsoon

At the mountainside,
a cluster of ash trees stood together.
For three or four days, the wind blew faintly,
then from morning, the sky clouded, and rain came.
All day, the rain came.

Each time my bare feet touch the bare floor,
my whole body is drenched in the sticky, clinging dampness.

On a clear, sunlit day,
I was planning a splendid flight
to approach you, soft and dry,
but today, the rain comes.

The vivid pink crape myrtle petals, soaked, bow their heads.
Are the crape myrtle petals the only ones hanging low?
The hesitation preparing for farewell flows away

with the rainwater.

Do not hesitate.
Letting go of all I so dearly longed for,
I, too, will flow away.

From toe to crown, soaked, I will flow away.
Into that deep water,
to you who will welcome me,
I will flow, wholly drenched.

저 석양의 단풍나무 좀 봐

어디서 어떻게 왔는지
그대 볼우물 깊이 파인
웃음의 파장인가 봐

잘게잘게 부서진 유리 이파리
파드득 햇살을 깨물었나 봐

깨진 빛살무늬
부르르 떨고 있어

붉은 치마 뒤집어쓰고
나는 그만 뛰어내릴 거야

유리창에 비친 저 살뜰한 그리움
조각조각 발에 밟혀
뚝뚝 붉은 지문 남기네

안녕
낡은 신발 한 켤레로 남은
저 석양의 단풍나무 좀 봐

Look at that maple tree in the sunset

Where it came from, how it arrived,
It seems like the ripples of laughter
Carved deep into your well of eyes.

The finely shattered glass leaves
Must have bitten the sunlight with a crunch.

The pattern of broken light
Is trembling faintly.
Wearing a red skirt upside down,

I'm about to leap off.
The tender longing reflected in the windowpane,
Crushed underfoot piece by piece,
Leaves red fingerprints, drip by drip.

Hello,
Look at that maple tree in the sunset,
Left as a pair of worn-out shoes.

철쭉 빛 저고리

뽀얗게 비누질한 고무신 속의
버선발이 토방을 밟는다

방문을 열고 나온 참이다
밖은 소소한 바람 불고

무슨 소식처럼 까치가 빨랫줄에 앉아 까악댄다

앞마당
복사꽃 배시시 웃음 짓는 아침

알 수 없는 슬픔이 밀려와
떠오르는 태양에 엇비친다

철쭉 빛 저고리 입은 여인네
태양을 등지고 넋 놓은 아침

The Azalea-Colored Jacke

The socked feet,
Slipped into freshly scrubbed rubber shoes,

Step onto the earthen floor.
Just stepping out from opening the door,

A gentle breeze blows outside.
Like some kind of news,
A magpie perches on the clothesline, chattering.

In the front yard,
The peach blossoms smile brightly in the morning.

An unknowable sadness wells up,
Reflected against the rising sun.

A woman in an azalea-colored jacket,
Lost in thought, her back to the sun in the morning.

첫눈

은빛 새들이 날아내린다
금빛 새들은 태양이 단죄하여 모두 내쫓고
은빛 새들만 사뿐히 날아내린다
태양은 자기를 닮아가는 새들을 시샘했나 보다
태양은 숨고 금빛 새들은 내쫓기고
은빛 새들만 태양을 밀어내고 있다

Silver Birds Descend

Golden birds, condemned by the sun, are all driven away,
While silver birds softly descend.
Perhaps the sun envied the birds that resembled it.
The sun hides, the golden birds are banished,
And only the silver birds push the sun aside.

청(青)

눈이 부서라
희디흰 발톱 세우고
주욱 뻗은 고양이 기지개 켠다

포르르 포르르
새의 깃털들
하늘 터는 소리 무심하고
소시민들 열쇠 꾸러미 절렁대며
광장을 내려와
자동차마다 열쇠 꽂고
부릉 떠나 버린다

모두 떠난 아파트 광장에
베기가스 매캐한 냄새뿐

내에앰새에뿌운

빈 유리문들은 눈이 부셔라
눈이 시려라

어슬렁어슬렁 광장에 떨어지는
조각난 금 부스러기
나무들은 잠깐 아무도 없는 사이
은근슬쩍 입술 비비고
그만 황홀하여라

찌일끔 낯 붉히는 꽃잎 수줍어라

광장 뒤쪽
나선의 계단을 밟으며
애인들은 층계를 오르고 또 오르고
꺄르륵 풀꽃들
한 무리 팔짱을 꼈다가 폈다가
어쩔 줄 몰라 쿨럭이는 잔기침 소리, 소리
이승의 꿈으로나
떠 돌아라
떠
돌아라

Blue

Dazzling to the eyes,
A cat stretches long, raising its white claws.
Purr, purr,

The rustle of bird feathers,
Indifferent, unmindful.
Townsfolk jangle their keychains,
Descending the plaza,
Each car key turned,
Roaring off with a rumble.

In the empty apartment plaza,
Only the acrid smell of exhaust lingers.

Faintly foul.
The empty glass doors dazzle,

Stinging the eyes.
Scattered fragments of gold dust
Fall lazily into the plaza.

The trees, in a moment when no one's around,
Secretly rub lips together,
Utterly enraptured.

제3부

바람의 속삭임
Whispers in the Wind

가을 산

산 능선을 기어오르는 길은 팍팍하다
때죽나무, 팥배나무, 상수리나무, 산벚나무
여름 내내 둥그렇게 몸을 말아 올리며
습기를 빨아들이는 동안
숲의 정기는 영글었나 보다
가끔씩 폐부 깊이 응혈된 흔적
발길에 채인다
살아온 만큼 버리고 간다
다시 길을 찾아 걸으면
산자락 밑에 한 그림자 숨었다 사라지고
들국화 한들한들 웃다가 말다가
두리번거리며 걸어가 보는 길
이제 가야 할 때가 가까워진다
예고된 긴 이별의 장강(長江)이
서산마루에 금니박이로 웃고 있다

Autumn Mountain

The path climbing the mountain ridge is rugged and unyielding.
Times of mulberry, wild pear, oak, and mountain cherry,
curling their bodies round through the summer,
sucking in moisture,
have ripened the forest's spirit, it seems.
At times, traces of congealed blood deep in the lungs
are stumbled upon underfoot.
What has lived is left behind.
Walking on, seeking the path anew,
a shadow slips beneath the mountain's hem, then vanishes.
Wild chrysanthemums sway, half-laughing, half-still,
as I tread, glancing around.
The time to depart draws near.
The foretold Long River of farewell,
gleaming with golden teeth, smiles atop the western ridge.

가을 소리

문 열고
하늘
쳐다보지 않아도
다 안다

스치듯, 사분거리듯
흐느끼듯, 울렁거리듯
출렁이듯, 흔들리듯
휩쓸리듯, 굴러가듯

밤새
성당의 높은
시계탑 위에서
두근두근
두근대는 소리

The Sound of Autumn

Opening the door,
I don't need to look up at the sky—
I know it all.

Like a brush, like a rustle,
Like a sob, like a quiver,
Like a ripple, like a sway,
Like being swept away, like rolling along.

All night long,
From the high clock tower
Of the cathedral,
A thumping,
Throbbing sound.

갈대

한 톨의 피
한 줌 움켰던 물

그마저
켜켜이 밀려오는
공명한 대기 속에
증발되면
비로소
나는 완성되어지려니
서걱서걱 그대들 가슴에 눕혀지려니

Galdae

A drop of blood,

A handful of water grasped,

Even that,

When it evaporates

Into the resounding air,

Layer by layer,

I shall be completed,

Rustling, to be laid upon your hearts.

그 섬에는 바람이

수시로 넘나들던 바람이
파도를 만들었다
때마다 운명의 섬들이 지어지고
섬의 윤곽이 다듬어질 때
바람은 다시 파도를 일으키고
부옇게 안개 낀 날에는
우리의 맑은 마음에도
작고 큰 일렁임이 출렁인다
층층으로 쌓여가는 안개의 덮개를 열어보면
잦은 바람에 작은 섬들이 점선처럼
지평선의 꼭지점에 다다를 것이다
꼬리에 꼬리를 무는 생의 미련을
가감 없이 떠나보낸 후 남겨진
그 섬에는 여전히 바람이 불고
파도가 철썩인다

On that island, the wind

The wind that constantly crossed over
Created waves
With each moment, islands of fate were built
And as the island's outline was refined
The wind stirred the waves again
On days shrouded in mist
Even in our clear hearts
Small and large ripples sway
When you lift the layered veil of fog
The small islands, carried by frequent winds,
Will reach the vertex of the horizon like dotted lines
After letting go, without restraint,
The lingering regrets of life that trail one after another
On that island, the wind still blows
And the waves crash.

눈의 정원

지난밤
우리가 잠든 동안
모든 집의 불이 꺼지는 동안
매화나무 매화가지는 꽃들을 피워내고

꽃인 듯 구름인 듯 하얀 길을
은여우들 우루루 달려갔는지
여우는 제 꼬리 열두 개쯤 감추고
제 털 뽑아 온 세상 은가루로 덮느라
제 몸 스스로 무덤이 되었는지

잠깐 결핍은 풍성해지고
뾰족뾰족 날 새운 것들 둥그렇게 몸을 말아
더러는 사탑(寺塔)이 되고 더러는 새로운 집이 만들어져
도로가 길게 늘어서고 솜사탕처럼 부드러운 도시에
눈이 내리네

새벽잠 깨운 눈 소리
왈칵 눈물나게 아름다운 하늘길 열어
어서 오라고 손짓하는

걸어서 걸어서 당도한 집
옴팍집

오롯이 같이 살아보자며
어깨 다독이는 당신
색 전등 켜며 깜박깜박
교신을 보내는

수수깡 삽짝문 밀치느라
잔뜩 꼬부린
내 등 위로
둥그런 무덤 하나 생겨나겠네

The Garden of Snow

Last night,
while we slept,
while every house's lights went out,
the plum tree's branches bloomed with flowers.

On a white path, like flowers or clouds,
did silver foxes race in droves?
The fox, hiding its dozen tails,
plucking its fur to dust the world with silver,
perhaps became its own tomb.

For a moment, scarcity becomes abundance,
sharp-edged things curl into rounds,
some becoming temple pagodas, others new homes.
Roads stretch long, and in a city soft as cotton candy,
snow falls.

The sound of snow waking the dawn,
opening a sky-path so beautiful it brings tears,
beckoning, "Come quickly."

The house I reach by walking and walking—
a sunken house.

You, patting my shoulder,
saying, "Let's live together fully,"
lighting colored lanterns, blinking,
sending signals.
Pushing open the reed gate,
over my hunched back,
a round tomb will rise.

만추

한낮의
풍경 속을 가다
문득 돌아서면

비둘기 발목으로
잠기는
눈 시린 빛 내리고

먼 강기슭
차오르는
비오리떼의

마알간 환청이
간간
흩어지는 들녘에

고개 숙여
무릎 꺾는
벼 이삭 소리

산그늘
아슴히 잠기는
산포도 내음

Late Autumn

Walking through
the midday landscape,
I suddenly turn back.

A dazzling light
sinks to the ankles
of a pigeon,

On the distant riverbank,
the rising flock
of wild ducks
casts a faint, crimson echo
across the fields,
scattering now and then.

The sound of rice stalks
bowing their heads,
bending their knees,

And the scent of wild grapes

faintly sinking
into the mountain's shadow.

엉겅퀴꽃

건넛방 섬돌에
벗어 놓은 신발 두 켤레

등짐 속 갯것들
가볍게 팔아넘기고
노을 진 언덕길
내려오다 마주쳤다네

눈웃음 살살 치며
꼬득였나

본 각시 씨앗 되어
형님형님 넉살 좋게
문 닫고 들어간 건넛방

히드득히드득
봉창문 사이로 들리는 소리

줄줄이 딸만 다섯 낳은
본 각시 탓하다

아들 하나 만들자고
또다시 키드득키드득

먼바다 한없이 바라보다
까무룩 정신 줄 놓치고
갯바위 언덕바지에 앉아
자기 가슴 콩콩 쥐어박던

본 각시 속 터지는
가슴애피* 꽃 피었다

*가슴애피 : 가슴통증

Thistle Flower

On the stone step of the opposite room,
two pairs of shoes are left behind.
The seaside goods in the pack
sold off lightly,
I met you coming down
the sunset-glow hill path.
With a gentle, teasing smile,
did you coax me?
Becoming the seed of the bride,
with charming, brotherly jest,
you entered the opposite room, closing the door.
Creak, creak,
sounds slip through the window frame.
Blaming the bride
who bore five daughters in a row,
to make a son,
once again, creak, creak:
Gazing endlessly at the distant sea,
losing myself in a daze,
sitting on the rocky hill's edge,

pounding my own chest.
The bride's bursting heart,
a thistle flower blooms in her aching chest

＊The term (chest pain) is translated as "aching chest" to maintain
 the emotional and poetic resonance of the original.

여름 바다

그 바다가 눈앞에 펼쳐졌을 때
내 가슴은 남몰래 출렁거렸지
먼 수평선으로 달아나며 달아나며
손 흔들던 그 여름 바다는
가지 말라고 아무리 말려도
흰 이빨 하얗게 드러내며 거품처럼 사라졌지
검은 바윗돌에 달라붙은 소라를
빈 소쿠리에 따 담다가
어쩔거나, 넋을 놓았는데
파도는 철썩이고
온몸을 뒤트는 여름 바다는
고동색으로 그을린 흔적을 남겨놓고
멀리 사라져버렸지
아직은 뜨거운 불씨들이
태양 아래 이글거리는데
먼 수평선에 줄을 긋는
긴 수염 늘어뜨린 해무의 무리들
석양에 붉게 젖은 옷깃 접으며
심통 부리듯 모든 흔적 잊으라 하네

Summer Sea

When that sea unfolded before my eyes,
my heart secretly surged.
Rushing, rushing toward the distant horizon,
that summer sea, waving its hand,
slipped away like foam, baring its white teeth,
no matter how much I begged it to stay.
Gathering periwinkles stuck to black rocks
into an empty basket,
I found myself lost in a trance.
The waves crashed,
and the summer sea, twisting my whole body,
left behind its scorched, conch-colored traces
and vanished far away.
The embers, still hot,
smolder under the sun,
while the sea fog, with long whiskers trailing,
draws a line across the distant horizon.
Folding its collar, dyed red by the sunset,
it tells me, as if sulking, to forget all its traces.

여름 환(幻)

빛의 함몰이네

사념은 야윈 바람을 몰아오고
영근 초록의 문 여는
눈과 눈 사이
짱짱한 유리알 유희였네

흥건한 빛의 몽상에서 깨어나
푸른 재채기 터트리는
야생의 벌판에
한낮은 기울어
심장이 멎을 듯 나른한 최면의 오후

달뜨는 마음 한 가운데
누군지 비늘을 털고 일어서는
하얀 갈기의 얼굴
암전의 시간은 가네

비밀인 듯 걸러낸
목숨의 불씨

비틀비틀 수혈을 감내한
빈혈의 강에 쏟아질
빛의 함몰이네

Summer Illusion

It is the collapse of light.

Idle thoughts drive a gaunt wind,
opening the gate of ripened green
between eye and eye,
a playful dance of sturdy glass beads.

Awakening from the drenched reverie of light,
a blue sneeze bursts forth
on the wild plain.
The midday tilts,
an afternoon of languid hypnosis, as if the heart might stop.

At the center of a moonlit heart,
Someone rises shaking off scales,
a face with a white mane.
The time of blackout passes.

Like a secret, sifted through,

the ember of life.

Staggering, enduring transfusion,
it pours into the anemic river,
the collapse of light.

저물녘 산사에서

 내가 아흔아홉 계단을 허적허적 숨 가쁘게 올라왔을 때 나는 섬세한 문양으로 지척거리는 무늬들의 문양을 보았다 무늬의 물결을 비껴선 나는, 무늬들이 날개를 파닥거리다가 그들의 내부에 음각된 어둠을 밀어 올리며 반사하는 햇살에 너스레 떠는 마지막 인사를 본다. 무늬들의 행렬은 저 백양나무 숲길로 바슬바슬 몰려와 무슨 슬픈 그늘을 쓸어내릴까

 아득히 석양을 등지고 울리는 범종 소리에 적벽(赤壁)으로 가는 내 몸은 파리하게 시들어 간다. 신발을 벗어 들고 신발 하나로 가벼워진 몸의 무게를 덜어내며 아흔아홉 계단을 한 계단 한 계단 밟아 내린다. 기척 없던 산사에 한차례 바람이 스치고 청솔모가 쪼르르 도망간 편백나무 가지 끝으로 가만 가만 산그늘이 보자기처럼 감쌀 때, 아래 마을 뒤편에 제일 먼저 환하게 불 밝히는 장례식장은 어제의 분망을 잃어버렸나 보다. 나는 서둘러 내려오는 산그늘을 피해 마지막 계단을 밟는다. 수천 년 마을을 감싸며 세월을 축적한 산이, 산 나무들의 무늬로 들어가고 있었다

At the Mountain Temple in the Twilight

When I climbed ninety-nine steps, panting and stumbling, I saw the patterns of intricate designs shimmering close by. Sidestepping the waves of patterns, I watched as they fluttered their wings, Pushing up the darkness engraved within them, reflecting the sunlight, Muttering their final farewells. The procession of patterns rustles Toward the poplar tree forest path, sweeping away some sorrowful shade.

At the distant sound of the temple bell ringing against the sunset, My body, heading toward the red cliffs, withers faintly. Taking off my shoes, lightened by the weight of one shoe, I descend the ninety-nine steps, one by one. As a breeze passes through the silent temple, And a squirrel scampers to the tip of a cypress branch, The mountain shade quietly wraps around like a cloth. In the village below, the funeral parlor, first to light up brightly, Seems to have lost yesterday's bustle. I hurry to escape the descending mountain shade, Stepping down the final stair. The mountain, embracing the village for thousands of years, Was entering the patterns of the mountain trees.

지는 목련꽃

한때는 예뻤다
잔설이 솜털처럼 몸에 붙어 떨어지지 않은 날
따스한 바람 한끝이 몸을 간지럽혔다
온몸이 간지러웠다
겨울 동안 꼭꼭 숨겨놓았던 몸을 풀고 고개를 쑤욱 내미니
모두 쳐다보면서 감탄했다
천상의 꽃이라고

천사같은 얼굴이 송이송이 피어났다
뭇사람들의 눈빛이 예쁘다 예쁘다 쓰다듬으며 지나갔다
바람도 쓰다듬었다
햇살도 쓰다듬었다
다들 한번씩 쓰다듬었으므로 몸살을 앓았다
천사처럼 웃던 얼굴은 점점 초췌해졌다
나중에는 '왜 저래'
짜증을 내면서 아무도 바라보지 않았다

The Fading Magnolia Blossom

Once, it was beautiful.
On a day when lingering snow clung to its body like soft fur,
A warm breeze tickled its edges.
Its whole being tingled.
Unfurling the body it had hidden tightly through winter,
It shyly stretched out its head,
And everyone gazed in awe,
Calling it a celestial flower.

찔레꽃 언덕

뽀얀 박명이다

내린천에
내린천에 솔솔 불어오는 바람
찬 이슬 밟으며 떨고 있구나

희미한 빛의 입자들
달빛 쏟아지는 밤 내내
종탑 위를 서성댄다

그렁그렁
흐느끼는 진주 빛 눈물 뿌리며
너는 오느냐
그대 영묘(靈妙)한 사고(思考)의 흰 피톨이여
난분분 난분분
휘날려라

The Briar Rose Hill

A soft twilight glow.

Along the down stream,
Along the down stream, the breeze gently blows,
Trembling as it treads on cold dew.

Faint particles of light,
All through the moonlit night,
Pace atop the bell tower.

Brimming,
Scattering pearly tears that sob,
Are you coming?
O white petals of your ethereal thoughts,
Fluttering, fluttering,
Drift and dance.

칠월 푸른 숲

모든 떠난 것들이 돌아와
넝쿨을 이룬다
귀엣말 속엣말 속삭이며
돌아와
이마 맞대고 어우러져
깊은 생성의 숨 비빈다
쭈욱쭈욱 기지개 켠다
뿌리는 뿌리들끼리
줄기는 줄기들끼리
엉키고 엉켜서
질편한 땅 위를 뒹군다
푸른 손바닥 뒤집어
하늘 끌어안아 잎사귀 떨린다
소나기 지나간 후
헹귀낸
마알간 바람의 말
-나는 꽃숨을 만들려 해요
전해지는 전언 속에
온갖 산 것들의 몸부림 뜨겁다
숲은 깊고 검게 익어서

툭툭 터져 수액 범벅인 산하
빛들의 화살촉에 번들대며
벌레들이 살찌는
칠월의 숲 푸른 숲

Blue Forest of July

All that has left returns,
Forming a tangle of vines.
Whispering secrets, soft murmurs,
They come back,
Foreheads touching, entwining,
Rubbing together the deep breath of creation.
Stretching long, languidly.
Roots entangle with roots,
Stems intertwine with stems,
Knotting and weaving,
Rolling across the lush earth.
Flipping green palms upward,
Embracing the sky, leaves tremble.
After the rain shower passes,
The rinsed,
Clear voice of the wind speaks:
—I will craft the breath of flowers.
In the relayed message,
The writhing of all living things burns hot.
The forest ripens, deep and dark,

Bursting with sap-soaked mountains and rivers,
Gleaming under the arrowheads of light.
Insects fatten,
In the blue forest of July, the verdant forest.

파밭길

싱그러워라
산그늘 걷히네
안개는 저만큼 나른히 숨 뿜어내어
헛손질하네
우리들 시야에
햇살 구겨지네
일상을 비껴서서
호미 한 손 쥐고 고적한 파밭 길 걸어보면
바삭바삭 대지에서 입술 트는 소리
새털구름은 엉덩방아 찧다가
소복히 알을 낳았나 봐
알들은 대궁이를 내밀고
부화를 꿈꾸었나 봐
늦봄 가뭇없이 따가운 햇살
은띠로 출렁이네
코끝에 매콤하게 맴도는 매운 내음
부화된 새 새끼
알궁둥이 내밀어 날아보려고
뒤뚱뒤뚱 안간힘 쓰나 봐

Green Onion Field Path

So fresh and alive,
The mountain shade lifts.
The fog, languidly exhaling,
Drifts aimlessly far off.
In our field of vision,
Sunlight crumples.
Stepping aside from daily life,
Holding a hoe in one hand, walking the quiet green onion field path,
The crisp sound of lips cracking from the earth.
Feather-light clouds, tumbling down,
Seem to have laid eggs softly.
The eggs poke out their sprouts,
Dreaming of hatching, perhaps.
In late spring, the relentless, stinging sunlight
Sways with a silver gleam.
A spicy scent lingers sharply at the tip of the nose.
Newly hatched chicks,
Pushing out their round rumps,
Wobble and struggle to take flight.

푸름에 대하여

어떤 그리움이 저리 드높이 떠올라
청청한 빛깔이 되었나
만상의 흐름은 짙어져
하늘을 푸르게 덧칠하고 있다
깊은 호숫가 그늘을 닮아가고 있다
아무리 육신이 깨끗하다 한들
어찌 영혼의 맑음을 따라갈 수 있으랴
영혼의 넋을 닦고 닦아
저만큼 올려놓았으니 하늘에 닿았다
맑은 날의 푸름에 대하여
우리 삶의 어지러움 속에서도
청정한 꿈을 꾸는 날은 희망이다

On Blueness

What longing rises so high
To become such a vivid blue?
The flow of all creation deepens,
Painting the sky with vibrant blue.
It comes to resemble the shadow of a deep lakeside.
No matter how pure the body may be,
How could it ever match the clarity of the soul?
Polishing and refining the spirit's essence,
It has been lifted so far it touches the sky.
On the blueness of a clear day,
Even amidst the chaos of our lives,
The day we dream a pure dream is hope.

제4부

엉켜진 대지
Woven Earth

가을 연가

은밀히 감추어 왔었다
내 살 속에 숨겨둔
가장 깊은 말들이
우수수 한숨을 쉰다

지난봄
그대 내 귓가에
설레이는 씨앗 하나 떨구더니
나는 그만 사랑을 앓았다

아무에게도 터놓지 못할
아픔의 방 하나 꾸미고
방문 두드릴 그대 그리다가
선홍열 앓는 어지럼병에 시달렸다

조금만 바람에 스치어도
청동의 눈
그리메에 젖어
머리칼마다 금빛 물드는 마술에 걸렸다

험한 세상
험한 길 헤집고 온
청동의 영혼
그대

나는 머리 흩트리고
그대 곁에 누워
방문 스치는 바람 소리 가득
슬픔을 깨문다

Autumn Love Song

Secretly, I had kept them hidden—
the deepest words buried in my flesh,
now sighing in a rustling cascade.
Last spring,
you dropped a trembling seed
into my ear,
and I fell ill with love.
Unable to confide in anyone,
I adorned a room of silent pain,
yearning for you to knock at its door,
tormented by the dizzying fever of scarlet longing.
Even the slightest brush of the breeze
sets my bronze eyes
drenched in yearning,
caught in the magic of golden light
weaving through every strand of hair.
O soul of bronze,
you who have wandered
through the harsh world's rugged paths—
you.

I let my hair fall loose
and lie beside you,
the sound of wind grazing the door
filling the air,
as I bite into sorrow.

가을 환(幻)

먼발치에 아득하네
뒷짐지고 돌아서서
떠날 준비
서두는 그대

맑은 빛 흔들며
뜨락을 내려와
잘 씻긴 나무들 비집고
서 있던 그대

최면에 취한 듯
가슴에 얼굴 묻었네

힘껏 껴안긴 팔에
막막한 비애 스며들면
점점 느슨하게 풀리는 팔
그만 헤어질 시간인가 봐

Autumn Illusion

From afar, you seem distant,
Turning away with hands clasped behind,
Preparing to leave,
You hasten your steps.
Shimmering in clear light,
You descend to the courtyard corona,
Slipping through the cleansed trees,
There you stood.
As if entranced,
You buried your face in my chest.
In the arms that held you tightly,
A vague sorrow seeps in.
The embrace slowly loosens,
It must be time to part.

넝쿨

어쩌면
바지랑대 위
저 끝
아슴히 떠 있는 고추잠자리
그 고추잠자리가 부러웠는지도 모르겠다

떠나간 사람은 돌아올 기미가 없고
수직으로 뻗은 천상의 길 한편에
벗어두고 간 구두 한 켤레

따라갈 수 없는 길목에
생목(生木)가지 아카시나무를 움켜쥔다

떠나간 사람이여
목숨을 말하진 않겠다
한해살이풀 우거진 풀덤불에
엉켜진 몸
주섬주섬 일어나
달랑 모가지 쳐들고
둘레둘레 둘러본다

곧바로 뻗은 저 직선의 길 놓아두고
구부러지고
휘감기고
휘청거렸다가
휘몰아쳤다가
가까스로 생의 길을 찾는다

Vine

Perhaps
I was envious
of the dragonfly
hovering faintly
at the end of the vine.

The one who left shows no sign of returning,
and on one side of the heavenly path
stretching vertically,
a pair of shoes left behind.

At the crossroads I cannot follow,
I clutch the living branch of an acacia tree.

Oh, you who have gone,
I won't speak of life.
In the thicket of annual grasses,
my body entangled,
I rise clumsily,
lifting my head,

and look around.

Leaving the straight path behind,
I bend,
I twist,
I stumble,
I whirl,
and barely find the path of life.

덕진 연못에 핀 연꽃

수만 번 경배하며
산천 곳곳에서
흘러와 모여들었다

강물처럼 매끄럽게
흐르지도 못하고
강바닥 모래톱 밀며
물웅덩이로 남아

때때로 바람불어
하늘이 뒤집어질 듯
스산한 날이면
치마 뒤집어 쓴 백제 여자들
풍덩풍덩 빠져들었었다네

그 후
남정네들 시절 따라
마음 내려놓는 날이면
날마다 여인들 받아내느라
내장이 썩어들어 그만 눈 감았네

눈 감지 마라
죽었던 백제 여자 다시 살아나
이토록 고고한 자태로
천리 밖까지
꽃향기 그윽하지 않은가

The Lotus in Deokjin Pond*

With countless bows of reverence,
they gathered, flowing in
from every corner of the mountains and rivers.

Unable to glide smoothly like a river,
they remain as pools of water,
pushing against the sandy riverbed.
On days when the wind howls
and the sky seems to overturn in desolation,
the women of Baekje, skirts flipped over their heads,
plunged into the water with a splash.

Thereafter,
when men, swayed by the times,
laid down their hearts,
the women, receiving them day after day,
rotted within and closed their eyes.

Do not close your eyes.
The women of Baekje, once dead, rise again,

blooming with such noble grace,
their fragrance wafting
a thousand miles afar.

* It refers to an artificial lake in Jeonju City.

무꽃

식민이 훑고 간 저탄 더미 아래
땅이 두텁게 마름질 되어 햇살에 반사된다
금강의 황토를 휩쓸고 온 바닷가 짠 갯벌에
뱀장어는 알을 슬고 장항 여객선 객실에 실려 온
인부들이 도선장을 떠나 선착장에 부려졌을 때
해망동 굴다리를 지나온 북쪽에서 온 피난민들은
무꽃 만발한 쌀 창고 옆길을 꽉 메워오고 있었다
일본으로 쌀을 실어 보내던 갯가에
개미 떼처럼 달라붙은 인부들의 어깨에
밀가루 부대 자루가 올려지고
선착장에 미군기 깃발을 펄럭이며 구호물자를 싣고 와
기세등등한 양코배기 앞에 늘 황송한 우리들
학교 급식 시간에 배당받은 우유가루를 입에 물고
우리들은 무꽃이 하얗게 핀 길을
군가를 부르며 집으로 돌아오고 있었다

Radish Flower

Beneath the coal heaps swept by the colonizers,
the earth, thickly parched, reflects the sunlight.
On the salty tidal flats by the sea, swept by the ochre of the Geum River,
eels lay their eggs, and laborers, carried in the cabins of the Janghang ferry,
are unloaded at the dock, leaving the pier behind.
Refugees from the north, passing through the Haemangdong underpass,
crowd the side paths by the rice warehouses, where radish flowers bloom in profusion.
At the shore where rice was shipped to Japan,
laborers, clinging like ants, hoist sacks of flour onto their shoulders.
At the dock, where the American flag flutters,
relief supplies arrive on swaggering foreign ships,
and we, ever deferential, stand in awe.
At school lunchtime, with powdered milk in our mouths,
we return home along the path where radish flowers bloom white,
singing military songs.

밤 부둣가

갈매기 날개 접고 잠든
파도 소리 철석거리는 밤 부둣가

낮 동안 질펀하게 목소리 큰 사내들이
내뱉고 떠난 억샌 말투 끊긴

점점 불어오는 밀물 차오름에
살찐 보름달이 환히 부푼다

장화 발소리 살금거리다
쓰레기 한 뭉치
휘익 던지고 떠난 자리

그 자리

갯벌에
옹기종기 잠들었던
갈매기들 푸드득 날아오른다

Night at the Wharf

Seagulls, wings folded, asleep,
The sound of waves clattering at the night wharf.

The coarse, loud voices of men
Spouting rough words during the day, now gone,

As the rising tide swells stronger,
The plump full moon glows brightly, swollen.

The cautious tread of boots,
A bundle of trash
Hurled with a whoosh, then abandoned—

At that spot,

From the tidal flats,
Seagulls, nestled in sleep,
Startle and take flight with a flutter.

변산 바람꽃

가을 앞세워
세찬 바람 불더니
떨어진 잎들은 저만큼 쓸려갔다

가을 가고
겨울 오는 길목에
바람만바람만 불어와
눈은 쌓여갔다

잠깐 멈춘 바람의 끝
살며시 고개 내민 햇살 따라
내리던 눈은 쌀밥처럼
고봉으로 쌓여가고

추위에 숨죽인 새들이
따스한 허공 속으로 날아오르다
그만 떨어뜨린 깃털들
양지에서 부르르 떨고 있다

산마루 모퉁이 끼고

볼우물처럼
수줍게 수줍게
꽃 우물 피워내고 있다

Byeonsan Windflower

Leading with autumn,
A fierce wind blew,

Sweeping fallen leaves far away.
As autumn left
And winter approached,
Only the wind, only the wind blew,
And snow began to pile.

At the brief pause of the wind's end,
Following the sunlight softly peeking through,
The falling snow, like steamed rice,
Heaps into high mounds.

Birds, hushed by the cold,
Soar into the warm air,
Dropping feathers
That tremble in the sunny patches.

Around the corner of the mountain ridge,

Like a dimpled well,
Shyly, oh so shyly,
A flower-well blooms.

실잠자리

물가 어스름 끝 그늘 드리운 연잎 그늘이 있어
꽁지를 오므리고 실낱같은 목숨 하루하루 잘 견뎠다

한때는
여름의 열기에 그만 꼬스라지는 줄 알았는데

툭 건드리고 날아간 여치가 옆자리에 날아와
찌르르 가을을 부른다

여름날 뜨거운 열정도 식은
푸른 하늘가 몽실몽실 흘러가는 흰 구름 떼
실잠자리 꼬리가 바람에 바르르 떨린다

Dragonfly

At the water's edge, in the twilight's end, beneath
the shade of lotus leaves, clutching its tail, it endured
day by day with a threadlike life.

There was a time
when I thought it would wither in the summer's
heat.

A grasshopper, brushing past and flying off, lands
nearby,
chirping to summon the autumn.

The fiery passion of summer days has cooled,
and under the blue sky, fluffy white clouds drift by.
The dragonfly's tail trembles faintly in the breeze.

어은리 염전

해롱해롱 고갯짓 싱그러운
버들강아지 머리 푼 언덕에서는
바다가 보였다
염전의 끝 길로 메마른 갈대 숲길이 이어지고
수십 년 불어오던 바람만 희끗거려 슬픈
빈 들판에 한숨인 양 바람 소리 소소하다
바닷물을 말려 희디흰 입자를 펼쳐
건져 올리던 그때는 행운이 뒤따랐다
구획된 구역마다 햇살에 하얗게 부서지던 소금입자들이
은화처럼 은빛으로 알알이 반짝이며 부(富)를 불러왔다
어느 날 생존에 적자를 덤처럼 얹어준
터전을 접고 떠난 자리에
까마득히 전설 같은 소문만 남고
휭휭한 바람의 막사 마당에 벗어 던진 면장갑을 뒤집으며
소금을 밟던 장화가 짝짝이로 굴러다닌다
마당 가득 웃자란 명아주는 개망초와 함께
바람 따라 허리를 꺾으며 춤을 추고
납작 엎드린 쇠뜨기풀도 덩달아 햇살을 움켜쥐며
엉그엉금 땅바닥을 기고 있다

Eoun-ri Salt Field

From the hill where fresh willow catkins sway,
their heads unbound,
the sea comes into view.
At the end of the salt field, a path of parched reeds stretches on,
and the wind, blowing for decades, whitens with a mournful sigh.
In the empty field, the sound of the wind whispers softly, like a breath.
Back then, drying seawater to spread fine white grains
brought good fortune in its wake.
In each divided plot, salt crystals shattered white under the sunlight,
glimmering like silver coins, each grain sparkling, calling forth wealth.
One day, burdened with the deficit of survival,
the land was abandoned,
leaving only faint legends and rumors behind.
In the barren yard of the wind's encampment,

a cotton glove, cast off, flips over,
and the boots that once trod the salt roll around, mismatched.
The yard, overgrown with lamb's quarters and wildflowers,
bends and dances with the wind,
while the prostrate knotweed, too, clutches at the sunlight,
crawling clumsily along the ground.

초봄

맨 처음
감추고 감추어 왔던
발을 벗어 보이고 싶었다
발을 내밀고
맨발로 너를 밟고 서 있으면
아직 녹지 않은 잔설이
발바닥 끝에서 곰실곰실 녹아나
내 오장육부와 핏줄에
환한 신호를 보내줄 것 같았다
연두의 휘장 흔들며
눈부신 사랑 하나
만들어 줄 것 같았다

Early spring

At the very first,
I wanted to bare the feet
I had kept hidden, concealed.
Stepping forward,
Standing barefoot upon you,
The lingering snow, yet to melt,
Would softly dissolve at the tips of my soles,
Sending a radiant signal
Through my organs and veins.
Swaying the pale green curtain,
It felt like it could craft
A dazzling love.

폭우

오늘 밤은 폭우다
참았던 울음들이 한꺼번에 목놓아 운다
한라산의 구상나무가 운다
월명산의 편백나무도 운다
가로등을 매단 벚나무도 운다

지구의 나날들은 견딜 수 없는 핍박으로 힘들었었다
지구의 꼭지들 화가 많이 났었나 보다

파고 헤집고 부수고
난리친 땅에 비가 내린다

먼 나라 열대 나무들
마구 베어냈었다
베어낸 땅에 불도 질렀다
한 산을 헐어내어
갯벌을 평평하게 메꿨다
지도를 바꿨으니 참 잘했다

강바닥 땅바닥을 뒤집어 제방도 쌓고 쌓았다

바다 밑 끝까지 추적하여 철근도 뚜드려 박았다
참 잘했다
우리들은 못할 일이 없다
달나라도 수없이 다녀왔는걸

달나라에서 수집해 온 먼지를 뭉치면
시멘트보다 몇십 배 강도가 높다지
그러니
이렇게 폭우라도 쏟아져야지
그럼 지구는 또 뒤집어지겠지

Torrential Rain

Tonight, it's a deluge.
The tears held back burst forth in a wail.
The fir trees of Hallasan weep,
The cypress trees of Wolmyeongsan weep,
The cherry trees holding streetlights weep.

The days of the earth have been heavy with unbearable oppression.
The peaks of the earth must have been seething with rage.

Crashing, tearing, breaking,
Rain pours down on the ravaged land.

Faraway tropical trees
Were ruthlessly cut down.
Fires were set on the cleared land.
An entire mountain was torn apart,
Flattening tidal flats.
The map was redrawn - well done, indeed.

Riverbeds and earth were overturned, embankments piled high.
Steel rods were hammered deep into the ocean floor.
Well done, indeed.
There's nothing we cannot do—
We've been to the moon countless times.

The dust collected from the moon,
When packed together, is said to be
Tens of times stronger than cement.
So,
A deluge like this must pour down.
And then, the earth will be turned upside down again.

현(絃)

가냘펏네

실핏줄의 떨림이 파장을 남기네
파장은 멈추지 않고 온몸을 더듬네
더듬거리던 촉각이 한 생애에 각을 맞대고 공중제비하네

잔잔한 바닷가 모래사장에 남긴 발자국
살짝 내려앉은 물떼새는
아장아장 무슨 소망을 남겼을까

건너 윗마을의 풍문을 몰고 온
양귀비꽃 지는 환각을 부르네
꺄옥! 꺄옥! 꺄옥!

물떼새들이 한순간 날아올라
현란한 군무를 출 때
느린 걸음으로 모래사장을 걷던 꽃게들의 옆걸음

화들짝 놀래키는
파도 소리
아득하네

String

So delicate.

The trembling of a fine vein leaves a ripple.
The ripple, unceasing, caresses the whole body.
The groping touch aligns with a lifetime, somersaulting through the air.

Footprints left on the quiet beach's sandy shore.
The sandpiper, lightly settling,
What wish did it toddle forth to leave behind?

Carrying rumors from the village above,
It calls forth the hallucination of fading poppy flowers.
Kyaok! Kyaok! Kyaok!

As the sandpipers take flight in a fleeting moment,
Performing a dazzling group dance,
The crabs, sidling slowly along the sandy shore,

Are startled by the sound of waves,
Distant and vast.

| 발문

오후 3시의 상상력 : 백승연의 시와 실존의 사막

최재진(Jay Choi)

거짓을 갈구하는 일상의 유혹

친숙했던 세상이 채워지지 않는 오후의 햇살 속에서 마치 신기루처럼 우리에게 그토록 낯선 모습으로 다가오는 경험은 무엇인가? 장바구니를 들고 집으로 돌아오는 주부, 자전거를 타고 바삐 내려가는 아이들, 힘들게 후진 주차를 완수하는 노신사의 모습 등과 같은 반복되는 일상적 장면이 오히려 섬광처럼 너무 낯선 풍경이 된다.

그 무엇이 되지 못한 나의/ 그 무엇이 되어/ 가을날 오후 3시에는:/ 낮은 키로 물구나무서서/ 그 무엇이 되고 싶었는데/ 그 무엇이 되지 못한/ 가을날 오후 3시에는

물구나무 서서 보는 세상은 어떤가? 그 세상은 여전히 그렇고 그런 곳일 수 있다. 하지만, 뒤집어 보는 세상을 마

주하는 시인은 놀랍게도 이렇게 말한다.

> 나는 금지된 사랑을 말하고 싶다/ 정적과 정적이 흐르는 단두대에서/ 모가지 툭 떨어트린/ 내란음모죄의 사형수를 사랑했노라고/ 말하고 싶다/ 가을날 오후 3시에는

전복된 세계에서 펼쳐지는 치열한 상상력은 다름 아닌 시인의 시가 펼쳐지는 무대이다. 아무 일도 일어나지 않을 것 같은 오후의 지루한 일상 속에서도 혁명을 꿈꾸는 상상력의 세계이다. 그것을 일탈이라고, 반역이라 부르건, 시인의 언어는 어느덧 우리들에게 질곡으로 다가오는 일상의 세계를 시적 상상력을 통해서 초월하려는 욕망을 말한다. 자잘한 삶의 결을 관찰하는 시인의 시선은 동시에 초월을 향해서 열려있다.

초월을 말하지만 백승연의 시선은 여전히 지금 그리고 여기에 머무른다. 백승연은 그렇다 하여 비루한 일상에서 탈출을 속삭이는 거짓된 낭만이나 구원의 신기루를 바라지 않는다. 거짓 구원의 달콤한 말들의 유혹을 거부하는 시인은 우리에게 무엇을 말해주는가? 간단히 답을 한다면 이런 실존의 공포에서 벗어날 아무런 대책을 주지 않는 것이다. 오히려 희망이 없는 또한 구원도 올 것 같지 않는 그런 세상은 우리가 건너야 할 사막을 노래한다.

거친 세상을 살아가기

> 뼈와 뼈 사이 열 강열하다
> 타다닥 뼛속 뜨거움 제풀에 열 받는다
> 사시사철 소금으로 말라붙은 틈
> 무거운 멍에 지고 푹푹 빠지는 희디흰 길 뻗친다
> 살면서 버팅겨준 하늘의 밧줄 칭칭 몸에 휘어 감고
> 살짝 지나가는 바람에도 흔들려 볼 일이다
> 풀어내고 풀어내어도 풀리지 않는 인연의 핏줄 끈질긴데
> 끈질긴 핏줄 산화시킬 사막의 바람 눈물 흘린다
> 흘린 눈물 빗방울 되어 간식처럼 깔깔하다
> 걸어도 걸어도 푹푹 빠져드는 모랫더미
> 굽어진 등 구부리고 허연 머리칼 산발한 여인 엎어진다
> — 사막을 건너는 법

사막을 건널 수 있는 길은 없다. 그저 다음의 발걸음 옮기는 것 만을 생각할 수 있다. 아니 어쩌면 애초에 사막을 건너는 것은 불가능한 꿈일지 모른다. 그러나 어쨌든 사막을 걸어나가야 한다면, 그것이 숙명이라면, 우리에게 어떤 선택이 남아 있는가? 언젠가 나타날 오아시스를 꿈꾸기 보다는

살면서 버팅겨준 하늘의 밧줄 칭칭 몸에 휘어 감고/ 살짝 지나가는 바람에도 흔들려 볼 일이다.

— 사막을 건너는 법

사막을 건너는 하나의 방법이 있다면, 그 가혹한 조건에서도 소소한 그러나 소중한 상상의 세계를 펼쳐보는 것이다. 그럴 때면 사막의 모래는 초원이 되고 사막의 바람조차 우리 귀에 속삭이는 밀어가 된다. 우리의 상상의 세계는 풍경을 바꾸는 연금술이 펼쳐진다. 세상은 그래도 견딜 만한 곳이라고 속삭여본다.

자연을 듣다

시인은 이 연금술의 눈길은 일상 속에 자연의 숨겨진 소리를 찾아내는 것이다. 자연은 그냥 우리 눈앞에 서있는 그런 존재가 아니라 애써 그리고 참을성 있게 귀를 기울이면 나타나는 그런 세계이다. 듣는 것은 기다림의 영역이다. 어쩌면 대책 없이 그저 기다려야 할지 모른다. 그런 행운이 찾아온다면 자연은 마치 종교적 계시처럼 우리에게 삶의 운율을 줄 수 있을지 모른다. 바로 이 지점에서 시인은 상상력의 연금술로 비밀스럽게 속삭여주는 자연의 소리를 감지한다. 파밭길의 소리를 들어보자.

싱그러워라
산그늘 걷히네
안개는 저만큼 나른히 숨 뿜어내어

> 헛손질하네
> 우리들 시야에
> 햇살 구겨지네
> 일상을 비껴서서
> 호미 한 손 쥐고 고적한 파밭 길 걸어보면
> 바삭바삭 대지에서 입술 트는 소리
> 새털구름은 엉덩방아 찧다가
> 소복히 알을 낳았나 봐
> 알들은 대궁이를 내밀고
> 부화를 꿈꾸었나 봐
>
> — 파밭길

 듣는 이에게 자연은 때로 그 소리를 내어준다. 그런 소리는 기적의 소리, 생명의 복음이다. 그러나 이런 듣기는 기적과 같은 행운의 모습으로 아주 드물게 찾아오는 경험이다. 시인은 그래서 자연의 다양한 소리에서 귀 기울이며 "사막을 건너는 법"을 배우라고 말하는지 모른다. 듣기 위해서 우리는 한사코 기다려야 한다. 그래서 듣는 것은 기다림의 다른 이름이다.

> 들어보세요
> 날마다 날마다
> 내 발목으로 차오르는 물소리를
> 들어보세요

시난밤 험한 산줄기 타고 내려온
찬 이슬이
내 뜨거운 이마에
푸른 우수의 알갱이로 떠돌 때
나는 그대 곁을 서성이며
가만가만 발돋음하였어요

— 물안개

 자연은 그렇기에 애써 기다리며 들어야 하는 사건이다. 여전히 시인의 놀라운 묘사의 연금술은 자연으로 감상적인 몰입을 허용하지 않는다. 다시 말하거니와 참으로 백승연 시인이 주는 고귀함은 그가 값싼 감성적 흥정과 시적 상상력을 타협하지 않는 치열함에 있다.

빈 집에 깃들기

바람이 시도 때도 없이 훑고 지나갔겠지

창문이 열리고 방문이 열리고
대문이 열리고
마침내 바람에 몽땅 털린 세간살이

사람의 온기까지
트럭 채 싣고 떠나버린
바람 숭숭한 집

다시 창문이 닫히고 방문이 닫히고
대문이 닫히고 대문 밖 자물쇠로 마무리된
울 밖으로 나팔꽃이 꿈처럼 피어있다

― 빈집

　세상의 모든 집들은 이미 빈집인지 모른다. 우리는 어느 순간에 그리고 어떤 장소에서만 그 집에 기거한다. 집은 그렇기에 우리에게는 너무도 친숙하지만 또한 너무 낯선 곳이기도 하다. 누군가 항상 살고 있지만 언젠가는 비워지고 마는 우리들의 빈집은 다름 아닌 실존의 가장 정직한 모습이다.
　자물쇠가 채워진 빈집의 담 밖에는 나팔꽃이 처연하게 피어있다. 시인은 굳이 그것을 꿈이라고 말해준다. 그래서 꿈을 꾸는 시인은 시를 쓰는 것이며, 우연히 그 빈집을 지나는 우리들은 시를 읽는 것이다. 한 번 만이라도 그런 빈집 앞에 걸음을 멈추지 않는 사람은 얼마나 궁핍한 삶을 사는 것인가?

| Appreciation

The Imagination of Three in the Afternoon: Baek Seung-yeon's Poetry and the Desert of Existence.

Jay Choi

The Temptation of Falsehood in Everyday Life

What is this experience that approaches us, so unfamiliar, like a mirage in the afternoon sunlight, within a world that feels both familiar and unfulfilled? The repetitive scenes of daily life - a housewife returning home with a shopping basket, children hurriedly riding bicycles downhill, an elderly man painstakingly completing a reverse parking maneuver - suddenly become as alien as a flash of light.

> At 3 p.m. on an autumn afternoon.
> What is the world like when viewed upside down? It may still be the same mundane place. Yet, the poet, encountering this inverted world, astonishingly declares:
> I want to speak of forbidden love,
> at the guillotine where silence flows with silence,

>   to say I loved the traitor sentenced to death,
>   whose head was severed for conspiracy.
>
>   —*At 3 p.m. on an autumn afternoon.*

In this overturned world, the poet's fierce imagination unfolds as the stage for poetry. Even in the monotonous routine of an uneventful afternoon, it is a world of imagination that dreams of revolution. Whether called rebellion or deviation, the poet's language speaks of a desire to transcend the oppressive weight of everyday life through poetic imagination. The poet's gaze, observing the minutiae of life, is thus open to transcendence. Yet, while speaking of transcendence, Baek Seung-yeon's gaze remains firmly rooted in the here and now. Even when immersed in the sordidness of daily life, Baek does not chase false romanticism or the mirage of salvation. Rejecting the sweet temptation of false promises of redemption, what does the poet offer us? Baek Seung-yeon's poetry provides no escape from the existential terror of this world. Instead, it portrays a world without hope or salvation—a desert we must cross.

Living in a Harsh World

>   Between bone and bone, the heat is fierce,
>   a scorching fire ignites within, burning itself out.

In every season, the cracks dry up with salt,
a heavy yoke weighs down, sinking into the blinding white path.
Bound tightly by the rope of fate, given by the heavens,
swaying even in the slightest passing breeze.
The ties of destiny, unyielding, cannot be undone,
and the desert wind oxidizes the tenacious bloodline, shedding tears.
The tears shed become raindrops, laughing like a snack.
Walking and walking, sinking into the endless pile of sand,
a woman with a bent back and disheveled white hair collapses.

—*How to Cross the Desert*

There is no path to cross the desert. All one can think of is taking the next step. Or perhaps crossing the desert is an impossible dream to begin with. But if we must walk through the desert, if it is our fate, what choices remain? Rather than dreaming of an oasis that may one day appear,

Bound tightly by the rope of fate, given by the heavens,
swaying even in the slightest passing breeze.

If there is a way to cross the desert, it is to unfold a small but precious world of imagination, even under such harsh conditions. In that moment, the desert's sand becomes a meadow, and even the desert wind whispers sweet nothings in our ears. The world of our imagination performs an alchemy that transforms the landscape. It whispers that the world is still a place worth enduring.

Listening to Nature

The poet's alchemical gaze seeks out the hidden sounds of nature within everyday life. Nature is not merely what stands before our eyes; it is a world that reveals itself only when we listen patiently and attentively. Listening belongs to the realm of waiting. Perhaps we must wait without any certainty. If such fortune arrives, nature might offer us the rhythm of life, like a religious revelation. At this very point, the poet, through the alchemy of imagination, detects the secret whispers of nature's sounds. Let us listen to the sounds of the onion field path:

> So fresh and green,
> the mountain shade lifts.
> The fog breathes lazily in the distance,

fumbling in vain.

In our field of vision,

the sunlight crumples.

Stepping aside from daily life,

holding a hoe in one hand, walking the solitary onion field path,

the crisp sound of the earth's lips cracking,

the feather-like clouds, stumbling and falling,

seem to have laid soft eggs.

The eggs stretch out their sprouts,

dreaming of hatching.

―*The Onion Field Path*

To those who listen, nature sometimes offers its sounds. Such sounds are the sounds of miracles, the gospel of life. Yet, such listening is a rare experience, a stroke of miraculous fortune. Thus, the poet may be telling us to learn "how to cross the desert" by listening intently to the myriad sounds of nature. To hear, we must strive to listen. And so, listening is waiting.

Listen,

day after day,

to the sound of water rising to my ankles.

Listen.

When the cold dew, descending from the rugged mountain ridge last night, wanders as blue grains of melancholy on my fevered forehead,

I linger by your side,

quietly standing on tiptoe.

—*Mist on the Water*

Nature, therefore, is an event that requires patient listening. The poet's astonishing descriptive alchemy does not allow for sentimental indulgence. To reiterate, the nobility of Baek Seung-yeon's poetry lies in its fierce refusal to compromise poetic imagination with cheap emotional bargaining.

Dwelling in an Empty House

The wind must have swept through recklessly, at all hours.

The windows open, the doors open,

the front gate opens,

and finally, the household stripped bare by the wind.

Even the warmth of people,

loaded onto a truck and taken away,

leaving a hollow, wind-swept house.

The windows close again, the doors close,

the front gate closes, locked from the outside,

and beyond the wall, morning glories bloom like a

dream.

—Empty House

All the houses in this world may already be empty. We reside in them only at certain moments, in certain places. A house is thus both deeply familiar and profoundly alien. Though someone always lives in it, it will one day be emptied. Our empty houses are nothing less than the most honest reflection of existence.

Beyond the locked gate of the empty house, morning glories bloom poignantly. The poet calls them a dream. To dream is to write poetry, and for those of us passing by that empty house, it is to read poetry. How impoverished is the life of someone who never pauses, even once, before such an empty house?

빈집
Empty House

2025년 10월 30일 초판 1쇄 펴냄

지은이 _ 백승연
펴낸이 _ 임인호
편집장 _ 김옥경
디자인 _ 장상호

펴 낸 곳 _ 도서출판 신세계문학
등록번호 _ 서울 종로 00200
주   소 _ 서울특별시 중구 퇴계로30길 24
대표전화 _ (02)6232-8356

ⓒ백승연, 2025
ISBN 979-11-964787-5-9 03810

* 지은이와 협의하여 인지는 생략합니다.
* 이 책 내용의 전부 또는 일부를 재사용하려면 반드시 지은이와
  도서출판 신세계문학 양측의 동의를 받아야 합니다.
* 책값은 뒤표지에 표시되어 있습니다.

* 이 시집은 한국예술인복지재단의 예술활동준비금지원사업의
  지원을 받아 발간되었습니다.

First edition, first printing: October 30, 2025
Author: Baek Seung-yeon
Publisher: Im In-ho
Editor-in-Chief: Kim Ok-kyung
Design: Jang Sang-ho
Published by: Shinseggyeo Literature
Publishing Registration Number: Seoul Jongno 00200
Address: 24 Toegye-ro 30-gil, Jung-gu, Seoul, South Korea
Phone: (02) 6232-8356

ⓒBaek Seung-yeon, 2025
ISBN: 979-11-964787-5-9 03810

By agreement with the author, the copyright notice is omitted. To reuse all or part of the contents of this book, permission must be obtained from both the author and New World Literature Publishing.

This poetry collection was published with the support of the Korea Artists Welfare Foundation's Artist Activity Preparation Fund Support Project.